Language: English

ISBN: 978-1-954531-33-8

Hopeful Minds

Hopeful Minds is a curriculum developed by Kathryn Goetzke, Founder of the International Foundation for Research and Education on ~~Depression~~ Hope (iFred) and CEO of The Shine Hope Company, alongside a group of Hope experts. The program is based on research that suggests Hope is a measurable and teachable skill. It impacts all outcomes in life, including academic and athletic performance, health, and resilience. Our aim is to equip children, educators, and parents with the tools they need to create, maintain, and grow Hope even during the most trying times.

Our focus is on prevention through practical tools and exercises. It is easily adaptable in different cultures through modifying stories and uses activities and examples to enhance lessons. Hope impacts an individual's ability to address economic challenges, environmental issues, job security, family relationships, and food security, so it is imperative to not underestimate the power of Hope.

The program is cyclical, using the sunflower as a continuous symbol for Hope. The sunflower is based on the rebranding work by iFred, focusing on universal symbolism to create a 'brand' for Hope. Please consider planting sunflower gardens or fields for Hope, creating artwork for Hope, or sharing our message and website to help others find their way to our program.

We are using the theory of a growth mindset to start building our future programs to show Hope in action, through presentations on the science of Hope, stories of Hopeful Heros, and strategies for Hope. We call it the 'how-to' of Hope, or Hope in action.

Please stay in touch by signing up for our newsletter at theshinehopecompany.com/hopebeat-weekly

TABLE OF CONTENTS

Hopeful Minds Definition List

The most important terms we use in our Hope curriculum, and that we Hope you will start using, include:

HOPE: We define Hope as a vision for something in the future, fueled by both positive feelings and inspired actions.

HOPELESSNESS: Hopelessness is both a feeling of despair and a sense of helplessness. It is emotional (a negative feeling) and motivational (an inability to act). We all experience moments of hopelessness and manage them with Hope skills.

POSITIVE FEELINGS: Positive feelings are those feelings that help us to stay hopeful as we work towards our goals.

INSPIRED ACTIONS: Inspired Actions are the deliberate steps you take to get in your upstairs brain and toward your goals in life.

UPSTAIRS BRAIN: This is where our thinking, imagining, problem-solving, and learning occur. This part of the brain is responsible for the development of sound decision-making and planning, control over emotions and body, and self-understanding and empathy. The upstairs brain is also where we access our positive feelings.

DOWNSTAIRS BRAIN: Also referred to as the reptilian brain, this part of the brain is responsible for basic functions such as breathing, blinking, heart rate, and fight, flight, freeze, or fawn mode. It is also responsible for the chemical stimulus associated with strong emotions, such as anger, sadness, and fear.

STRESS RESPONSE: Your stress response is when an external or internal trigger causes your brain to release stress hormones, such as cortisol, adrenaline, and norepinephrine, that force you into your fight, flight, freeze, or fawn mode. It generally lasts 90 seconds from time of the last trigger.

STRESS SKILLS: These are actions that help you navigate your stress response and work through your body's chemical response to external stimuli, to manage your downstairs brain and get you back upstairs.

HAPPINESS HABITS: These are healthy, long-term habits that help you stay in your upstairs brain, where you access the problem-solving skills, collaboration, and passion critical for Hope. When you take time for Happiness Habits, your brain releases happiness hormones, such as endorphins, dopamine, serotonin, and oxytocin.

NOURISHING NETWORKS: Your Nourishing Networks are the Hope Networks of the people in your life that provide you with support, help you stay on track, encourage you to succeed, and who you do the same for in return.

ELIMINATING CHALLENGES: Challenges to Hope are negative thinking patterns, like limiting beliefs, automatic negative thoughts, all-or-nothing thinking, negative bias, rumination, worry, focusing on uncontrollables, attaching to outcomes, and internalizing failure, that can keep us in hopelessness states. Eliminating challenges is the conscious act of using Hope skills to overcome these challenges and get back to Hope.

THE HOPE MATRIX: The Hope Matrix is the process that we use to get from hopelessness to Hope. The Hope Matrix teaches us that to cultivate Hope, we must move from despair to positive feelings, and from helplessness to inspired actions.

SHINE HOPE™: This is the mnemonic we use to remember our Hope skills. Shine stands for: Stress Skills, Happiness Habits, Inspired Actions, Nourishing Networks, and Eliminating Challenges and is what we use to activate skills for Hope.

As you engage with the materials, we kindly request that you share the images from your Hope guide on social media. This will aid us in learning and motivating others on the art of Hope. Please tag @ifredorg and @theshinehopecompany, and include the designated hashtags #Hope #hopefulminds #ShineHope. If you are a younger user, please obtain parental permission before posting on social media. We appreciate your commitment to embracing Hope not just for yourself, but for those you influence and educate. Together, we can improve our collective future; Hope is key to creating all we want.

Pre-Lesson: Creating a Habit for Hope

Creating any new habit takes effort, commitment, and patience. It's not always easy, but with consistent practice and a clear understanding of why it matters to you, growth becomes possible—even in the face of challenges.

Think about this: If you were asked to run a mile today, how would that feel? Could you do it? Now, imagine running a mile every single day. Over time, it would likely become easier, and eventually, it might even feel natural.

That's what we Hope to achieve with learning Hope. We want the skills of Hope to become a part of your daily life—something that feels natural and automatic. Learning anything new can feel overwhelming at first, so before we dive in, take a moment to reflect on what's motivating *you* to be here.

Why do you want to build the skills to strengthen Hope? Why is this important to you? (Take a moment to write your thoughts—be as specific as possible!)

Now, go a little deeper—what is your why behind that?

And what is your why behind that?

When challenges arise, what will help you stay committed to this learning?

Keep these reflections close. Research shows that people are much more likely to achieve a goal when they write it down. By taking the time to reflect and write today, you've already taken an important step toward making Hope a lasting part of your life.

Lesson 1
The Science of Hopelessness

As we move higher on the Positive Feelings and Inspired Actions axes, we move toward "high Hope". This is why it's important to build our skills on both axes.

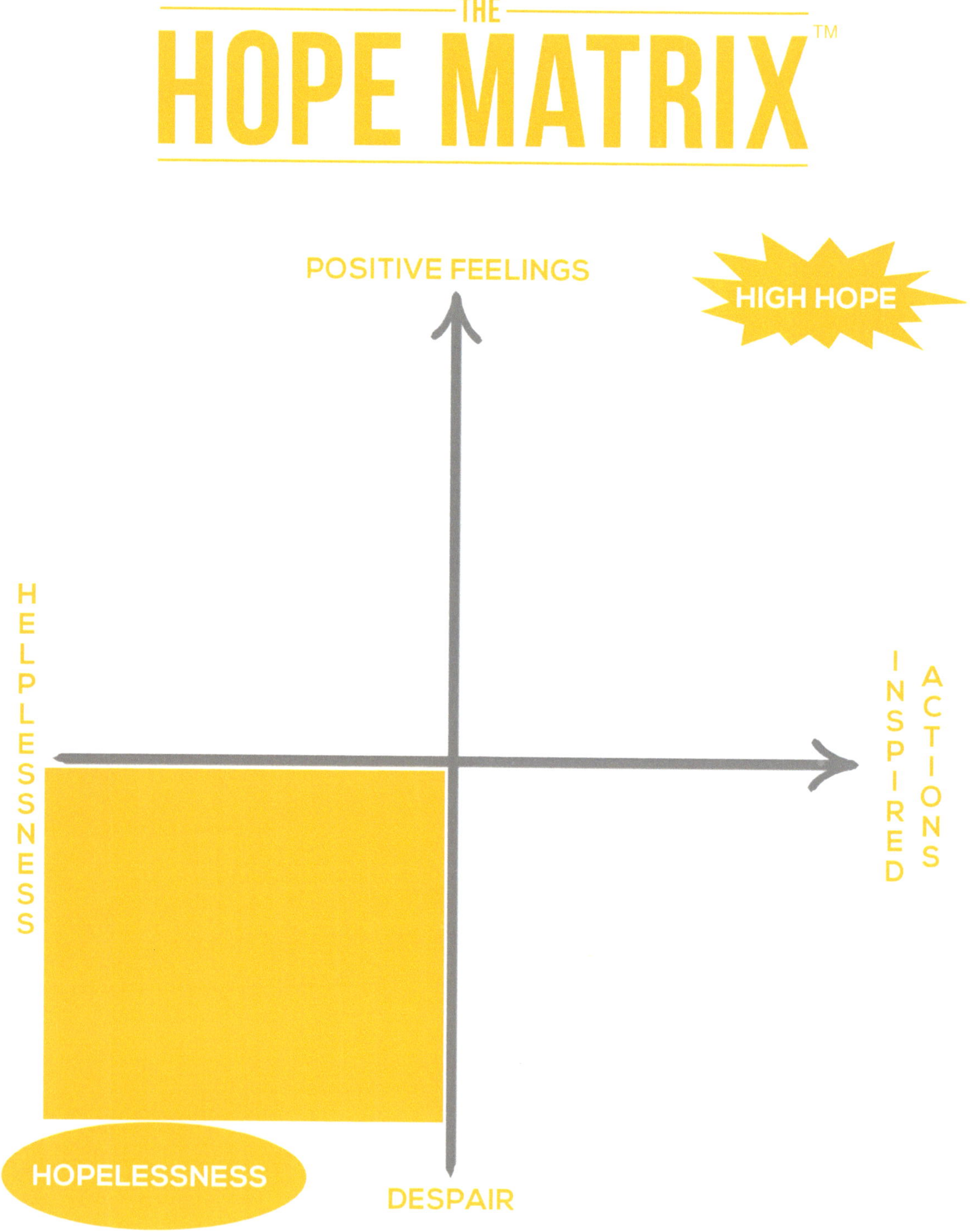

THE
HOPE MATRIX™

POSITIVE FEELINGS

HIGH HOPE

HELPLESSNESS

INSPIRED ACTIONS

HOPELESSNESS

DESPAIR

Objectives

- Identify the two ingredients of hopelessness (despair and helplessness) using The Hope Matrix.
- Understand that hopeless moments are normal, and know they can be navigated using Shine Hope Skills.
- Be able to identify three moments of hopelessness (big or small).

Pre-Questions

What is your definition of hopelessness? (Make sure it includes both emotions and motivations, i.e. sadness and stuckness)

>

What do you think are the common causes of hopelessness?

>

What would make someone more resilient to hopelessness than others?

>

Lesson Instructions

Moments of hopelessness are normal and a part of everyday life for everyone. To manage hopelessness healthily, we must first recognize what it looks like. Hopelessness is comprised of two key ingredients: despair (negative emotions) and helplessness (a sense of powerlessness).

Looking at the Hope Matrix, we can see that the ingredients of hopelessness are on a continuum. On one end, we have despair; on the other, we have positive feelings. Looking at the second ingredient, we have helplessness on one end, and on the other, we have inspired actions. Looking at the matrix as a whole, we can see that hopelessness (lower left quadrant) arises when both despair and helplessness are present.

Physical Activity

Let's act out the ingredients to hopelessness.

1. Despair consists of three primary emotions: anger, sadness, and fear. As humans, it is normal to experience these emotions. Take a moment to think about how your body looks when you experience:
   - Anger
   - Sadness
   - Fear

   Take turns showing what your body looks like when you experience one of these emotions. Talk through what you feel internally (i.e., tension, uneasiness, etc.) and where you feel it. The group will guess which one of the emotions each person is acting out.

2. Helplessness is when we feel powerless to do anything. We aren't motivated and can't act. Take turns demonstrating what helplessness looks like.

   When we experience emotions like sadness, anger, and fear, but feel motivated and know we have power, we can healthily move through the emotions. We can find solutions to challenges when we feel helpless but have a positive mindset. The combination of both emotional despair and motivational helplessness is the cause of hopelessness and can prevent us from overcoming the challenges we face.

3. What do both emotional despair and helplessness look like for you? Show us through your body language and talk through where and what you feel in your body. What might make us feel this way?

Arts and Crafts

Let's draw out the ingredients of hopelessness. You can use lines, edges, colors, portraits, images, shapes, or emojis. Whatever you prefer. (2 mins for each)

Despair

Draw what anger looks like

Draw what sadness looks like

Draw what fear looks like

Combine these drawings into one that represents despair.

Helplessness

Draw what being unable to act looks like

Draw what powerlessness looks like

Combine these drawings into one that represents helplessness.

Hopelessness

Draw a combination of your drawings of both despair and helplessness to create a symbol for hopelessness.

Recap Questions:

How do emotional despair and helplessness look different?

[ ]

What can cause someone to experience hopelessness?

Small Things

[ ]

Big Things

[ ]

Based on the activities, what are the themes for how someone can recognize moments of hopelessness in themselves?

[ ]

Now you know what hopelessness is. The good news is that you can always manage it. We want to ensure everyone can manage hopelessness because, left unresolved, it can become persistent and have major impacts on mental and physical health. Luckily, there is always a way to get to Hope, and the Shine Hope Skills are here to help us do just that. In the next lesson, we will learn how to Shine Hope.

Lesson 2
The Science of Hope

THE
HOPE MATRIX™

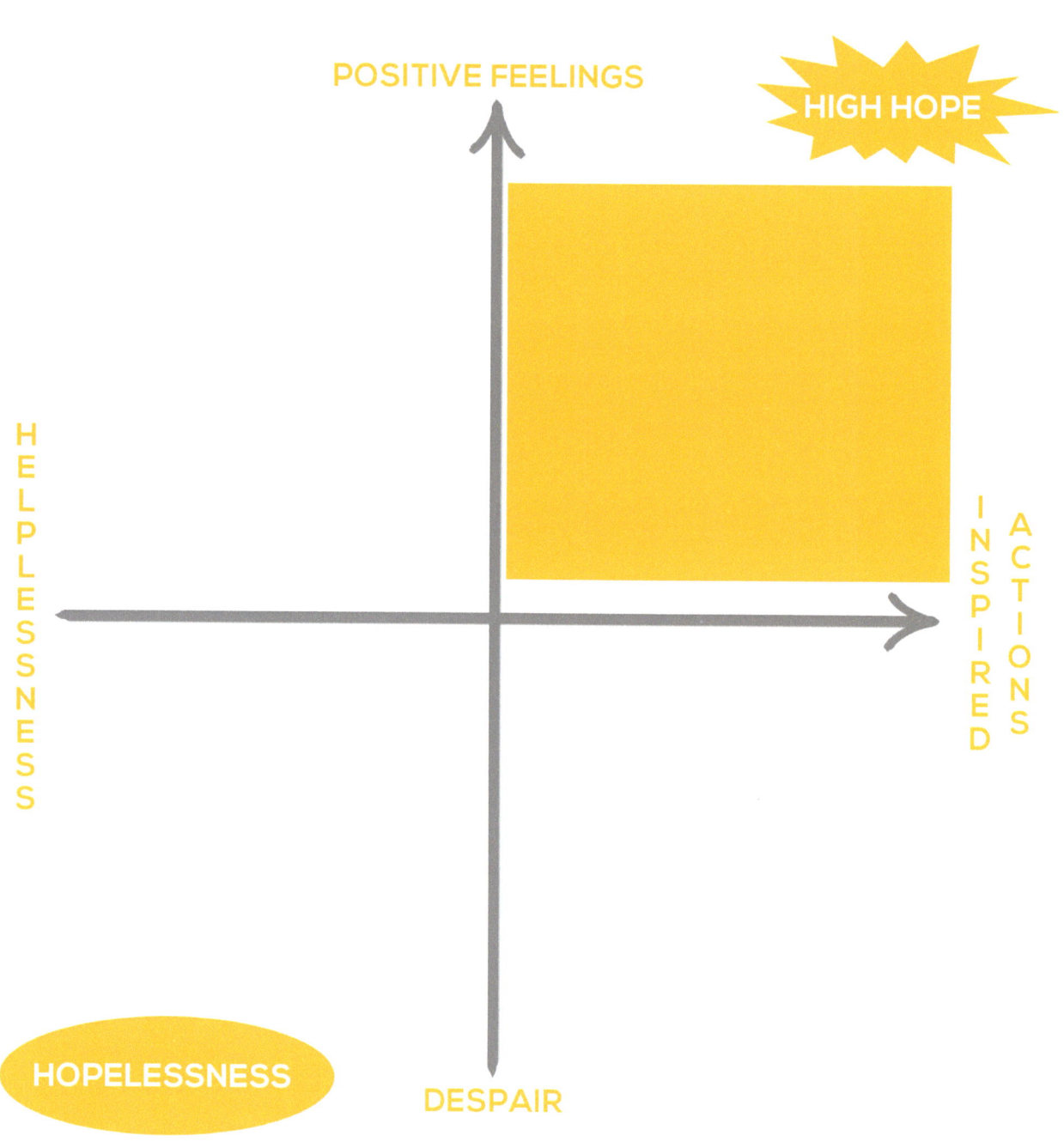

POSITIVE FEELINGS

HIGH HOPE

HELPLESSNESS

INSPIRED ACTIONS

HOPELESSNESS

DESPAIR

Objectives

- Identify the two ingredients of Hope: positive feelings and inspired actions.
- Identify the Five Keys to Shine Hope.
- Explain three reasons why Hope is important in life.

Pre-Questions

What is your definition of Hope?

What role do you think Hope plays in overcoming challenges?

What makes Hope important? (how long you live, how well you do in tests, in sports, etc.)

Lesson Instructions

To define Hope, we need to think back to our definition of hopelessness (emotional despair and motivational helplessness). We use The Hope Matrix to illustrate the movement from hopelessness to Hope.

Looking at The Hope Matrix, what words best describe the opposite of despair and helplessness?

Kathryn Goetzke, the creator of this program, defined Hope based on an understanding of the opposite of Hope: hopelessness (emotional despair and helplessness). She defines Hope as a "**Vision for something in the future** fueled by *positive feelings* and *inspired actions*." To navigate moments of hopelessness and move to Hope, we must shift from despair to positive feelings and from helplessness to inspired actions.

While she has come up with this definition of Hope, she also believes everyone can create their own definition of Hope, as long as it includes the two main ingredients: positive feelings and actions! Without action, Hope is just a wish!

She proved her theory that you could teach Hope using scientific methods and created The Five Keys to Shine Hope as an easy way to remember 'how' to Hope. Shine is a mnemonic for Stress Skills, Happiness Habits, Inspired Actions, Nourishing Networks, and Eliminating Challenges. The more challenges we have, the more we have to Shine!

Physical Activity

Let's act out the ingredients of Hope.

1. What emotions come up when you think about positive feelings? These might include emotions like excitement, joy, love, happiness, and many more. Take a moment to think about how your body looks when you experience these emotions.
2. Now, take turns showing what your body looks like when you experience one of these emotions. Talk through what you are feeling internally (i.e., release, warmth, etc.) and where you feel it in your body. The group will guess which emotion each person is acting out.
3. Inspired Actions are the intentional steps or behaviors we take to achieve our goals. Take turns demonstrating what inspired actions look like for you. When we feel positive emotions but lack motivation to work toward our goals, we may engage in risky or unhealthy behaviors. Similarly, when we take Inspired

Actions without experiencing positive emotions, we can also be drawn toward risky behaviors. To effectively move from hopelessness to Hope, we need a balance of both positive emotions and Inspired Actions.

4. What do both positive feelings and Inspired Actions look like for you? Show us through your body language and talk through where and what you feel in your body.

Arts and Crafts

Let's draw out the ingredients of Hope. You can use lines, edges, colors, portraits, images, shapes, or emojis. Whatever you prefer. (2 mins for each)

Positive Feelings (you can choose your own or use the recommendations below):

Draw what happiness looks like	*Draw what joy looks like*
Draw what love looks like	*Combine these drawings into one that represents positive feelings.*

Inspired Actions

Draw what motivation looks like

Draw what working toward goals looks like

Combine these drawings into one that represents Inspired Actions

Hope

Draw a combination of your drawings of both positive feelings and Inspired Actions to create a symbol for Hope.

Recap Questions:

How are positive feelings and inspired actions different?

Based on the activities, how can one recognize Hope within themselves?

What can people do to cultivate or strengthen their sense of Hope?

Lesson 3
Stress Skills

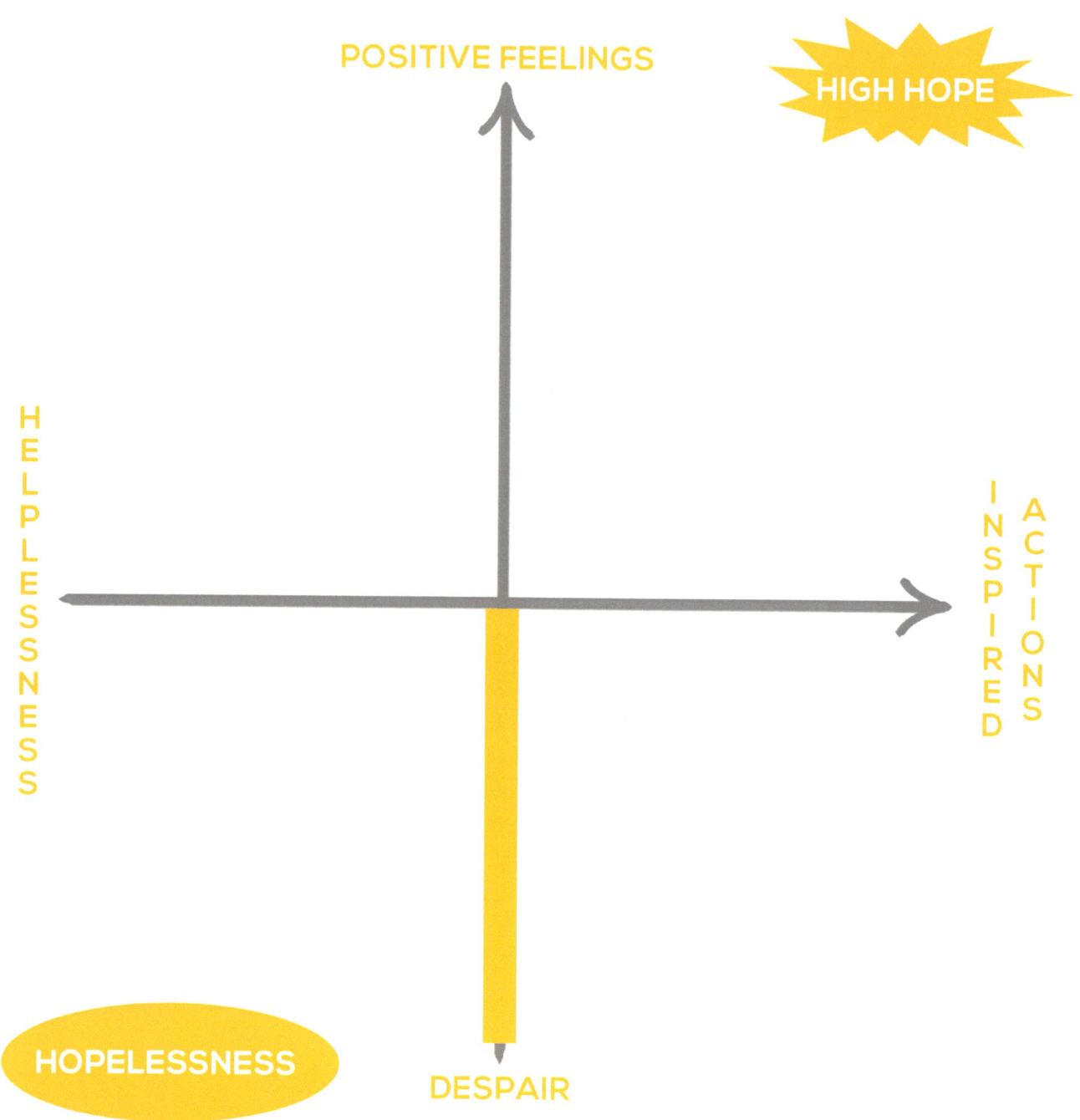

POSITIVE FEELINGS

HIGH HOPE

HELPLESSNESS

INSPIRED ACTIONS

HOPELESSNESS

DESPAIR

Objective

- Explain the concepts of the upstairs and downstairs brains and their roles in managing stress.
- Understand the stress response and apply the 90-second rule to regulate emotional reactions.
- Identify and practice three practical stress management skills.

Pre-Questions

What does stress feel like for you?

[ ]

Do you know the four responses someone can have to extreme stress?

[ ]

The stress responses happen in 1/20 of a second and are an automatic bodily process.

Fight: *the instinct to aggressively confront a threat. It can look like irritability, anger, or aggression in response to a trigger.*

Flight: *The instinct to run away or hide from a threat. It can look like panic, avoidance, anxiety, and fear.*

Freeze: *Numbness or inability to act or respond to a threat. It can look like disassociation, collapse, or signs of depression.*

Fawn: *The instinct to appease or comply with the threat to avoid conflict. It can look like compliance, people-pleasing, or difficulty saying "no".*

What are everyday situations that make you feel stressed?

On a scale from 1-10, how effective do you think your current stress management strategies are? What led you to choose this number?

Do you have any goals regarding how you want to manage stress in your life?

Lesson Instructions

Stress Skills, the "S" in Shine, help you manage negatively charged emotions. We often experience negatively charged emotions during moments of hopelessness, and it's essential to develop strategies to manage those emotions to help cultivate Hope.

The Upstairs and Downstairs Brain are concepts that help explain how our brain processes emotions and decision-making.

The Upstairs Brain (prefrontal cortex) is responsible for thinking, problem-solving, and self-control. It helps us make rational decisions and regulate emotions.

The Downstairs Brain (amygdala, limbic system, and brainstem) controls survival instincts, emotions, and automatic reactions like fight, flight, or freeze. It kicks in when we feel threatened or overwhelmed.

When stressed, the downstairs brain can take over, triggering our fight, flight, freeze, or fawn response and making it hard to think clearly. Our ancestors relied on the downstairs brain to keep them safe when confronted with dangerous situations. This response has been passed down through generations, but sometimes it malfunctions, triggering that fight, flight, freeze, or fawn signal due to perceived danger even when no real threat exists.

When we are in the downstairs brain, we may feel increased anger or stress; when we experience these emotions, it's impossible to feel happy. Our downstairs brain makes it challenging to think, problem-solve, or communicate with others.

The good news is that we can learn to take more control over our downstairs brain by strengthening our upstairs brain. Our goal is to move back into the upstairs brain when we are in the downstairs brain. When we strengthen our upstairs brain through coping skills, we can work to manage stress more effectively rather than act impulsively.

One strategy for regaining control using the upstairs brain is to follow the 90-second rule. This rule states that when we experience a strong emotion, the physical reaction of fight or flight (like increased heart rate) lasts about 90 seconds. After that, the body starts returns to normal unless another trigger prolongs the response.

By recognizing that the physical reaction is temporary, we can pause and feel the response for 90 seconds before responding to the trigger. Allowing this time to pass helps us process the stress response rather than avoid it, reducing the chance of reinforcing the same reaction in future situations.

Physical Activity

Let's practice the 90-second pause. This activity helps reinforce that the physical symptoms that often accompany our stress response are temporary and by pausing, we can allow our brain and body to reset before reacting. These physical symptoms can feel very similar to what our body does when we exercise, but it's important to note that the stress response includes unhelpful thinking patterns (i.e., worries, rumination, automatic negative thoughts) with the physical symptoms. In this activity, we only practice using the physical symptoms to demonstrate how quickly the body can come down after a trigger.

Step 1: Increase Your Heart Rate (60 seconds)
- Engage in a short burst of physical activity to simulate a stress response
  <u>Choose one:</u>
  - Do 30 seconds of jumping jacks.
  - Run in place as fast as you can.
  - Punch the air.
- After 60 seconds, stop and notice how your body feels—your heart rate is up, and you may feel breathless or tense. These sensations mimic the physical sensations your body may have as an immediate reaction to stress as part of the fight-or-flight response.

Step 2: The 90-Second Pause
- Take slow deep breaths.
- Observe without reacting: Notice your heartbeat slowing down and your body calming.

Step 3: After 90 seconds, check in with yourself:
- Do you feel calmer?
- Did your body naturally begin returning to baseline?
- How does this apply to stressful situations in everyday life?

Arts and Crafts

Let's draw the upstairs and downstairs brains. Take a piece of paper and fold it in half, with one side representing the upstairs brain and the other representing the downstairs brain.

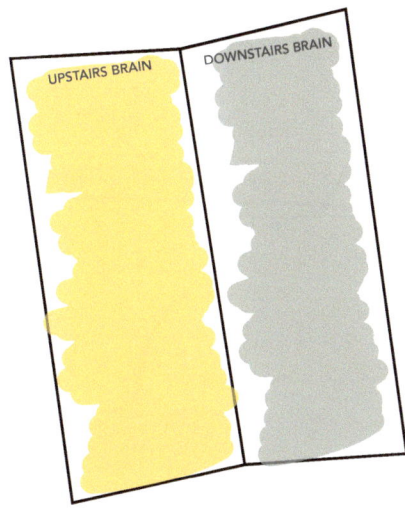

- Color each side differently.
- Illustrate the part of each brain section:
  - **Upstairs brain:** Draw or write things like problem-solving, self-control, and stress skills. Write a list of your top 5 favorite stress skills that you've tried before or would like to try.
  - **Downstairs brain:** Draw or write bad decisions, big emotions, fight, flight, freeze, fear, anger, sadness, and impulsive reactions.

Recap Questions:

How do the upstairs brain and downstairs brain differ?

How can you recognize when you should take a 90-second pause?

What are some stress skills that people can use to move from the downstairs brain to the upstairs brain?

UPSTAIRS AND DOWNSTAIRS BRAIN

FOLD HERE

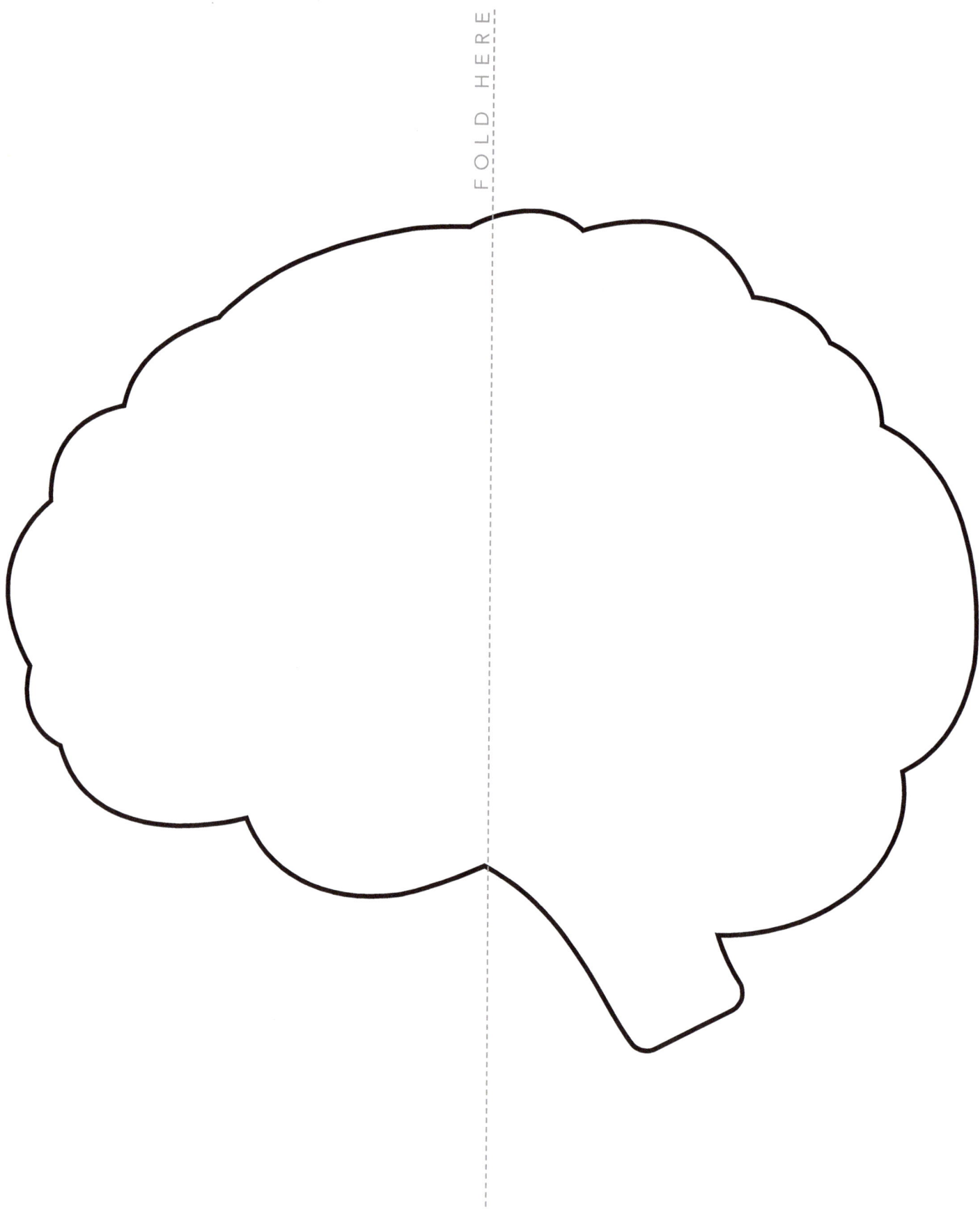

Lesson 4
<u>H</u>appiness Habits

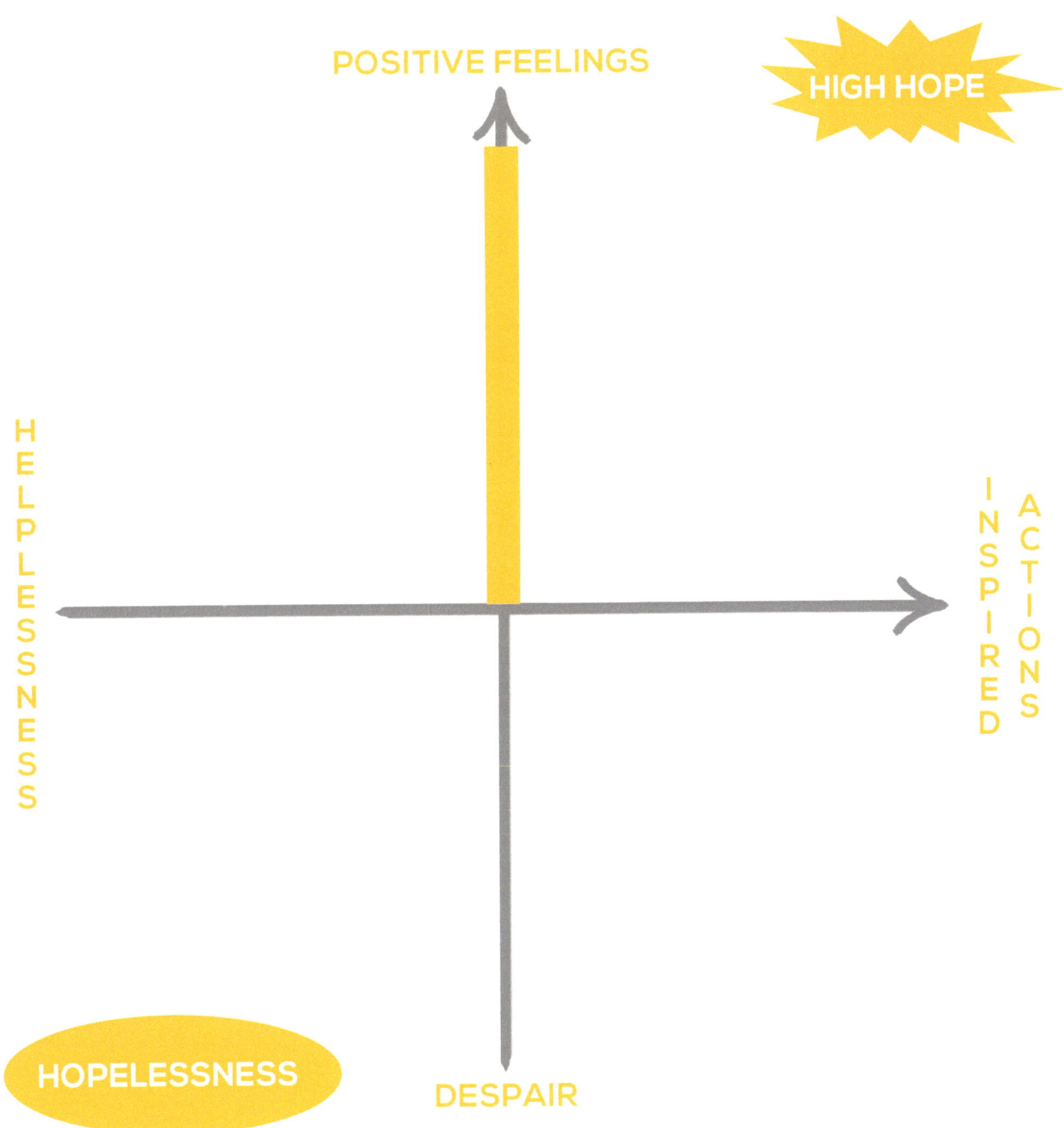

POSITIVE FEELINGS

HIGH HOPE

HELPLESSNESS

INSPIRED ACTIONS

HOPELESSNESS

DESPAIR

Objective

- Identify three healthy Happiness Habits
- Understand the meaning of staying in your upstairs brain and how it relates to emotional regulation and decision-making
- Know the role of Happy Hormones and recognize behaviors that induce happiness hormones in the body

Pre-Questions

How often do you engage in an activity that contributes to your happiness? What stops you from engaging in the activity more?

What are some activities or experiences that cause you to feel happy?

What do you think gets in the way of happiness?

Lesson Instructions

Happiness Habits, the "H" in Shine, are skills that help maintain positive feelings. If we consistently practice the Happiness Habits that keep up in the upstairs brain, we are less likely to experience lasting negatively charged emotions.

Happiness Habits are healthy, long-term actions that foster positive feelings and keep up in our "upstairs brain." Positive feelings help cultivate Hope and encourage movement toward our goals. As with any habit, we need to make sure we practice our Happiness Habits regularly to boost Hope and protect against unpleasant emotions.

When we practice Happiness Habits, several key brain hormones and neurotransmitters come into play.

Endorphins: reduce stress and pain and are released through exercise, gratitude, and laughter.
Dopamine: acts as the "reward" neurotransmitter, and higher quantities are available in our brains when we set goals and achieve them.
Serotonin: boosts mood and stabilizes mood; it's released with the practice of gratitude and mindfulness.
Oxytocin: strengthens social bonds and is released through kindness and connection.

Too much or too little of any hormone or neurotransmitter can create problems. To some degree, we have control over releasing of neurotransmitters and hormones through safe and unsafe activities. Below we've presented a few safe and unsafe activities for each neurotransmitter or hormone.

Neurotransmitter/ Hormone	Safe	Unsafe
Dopamine • Part of the reward system, or process in the brain that connects an event to a positive reward like happiness • Increases motivation and concentration	• Healthy diet • Creative activities • Protected sunlight exposure • Accomplishing goals	• Drug/alcohol use • Excessive social media use • Risky behaviors (i.e., reckless driving, harm to oneself)
Serotonin • Helps with learning and memory • Helps regulate mood, making us feel emotionally stable, happier, and calmer	• Adequate sleep • Acts of kindness • Socializing • Expressing gratitude • Mindfulness	• Over-reliance on social media for validation • Overeating • Drug/alcohol use
Endorphins • Help reduce stress by promoting relaxation • Plays a role in social bonding and connections • Acts as a natural painkiller and induces feelings of happiness and well-being	• Exercise • Hugs • Spending time in nature • Dancing	• Compulsive shopping • Violence • Risky sexual behaviors
Oxytocin • Helps with social bonding and is linked to feelings of trust • Has a calming effect, reducing stress and anxiety levels • Linked to altruism and generosity	• Social interaction • Laughter • Pet interaction	• Risky sexual behaviors • Unhealthy relationships

Physical Activity

Let's practice Happiness Habits through a Relay Race / Happiness Lab

- Set up stations that each represent a Happiness Habit (e.g., exercise, mindfulness, laughter, gratitude, etc.). Choose habits that make sense for the group's ability. Split the group into two teams and have them line up at the starting point. Have one person from each team complete an activity at one station of their choosing before tagging in their teammate.
- Here are some example stations; however, these can easily be adapted to meet the unique needs of the population working through the program:
  - **Gratitude:** Talk about one person you are grateful for and provide a specific example of what they did and how it made you feel.
  - **Mindfulness Walk:** Walk slowly for five steps, take two deep breaths, and highlight three things from your surroundings. (Alternative: take five deep breaths and notice five sounds you can hear.)
  - **Exercise:** Run in place, punch the air, or quickly clap your hands for ten seconds.
  - **Laughter challenge:** Tell a joke, make a silly face, or do a fun pose to make someone else smile.

Arts and Crafts

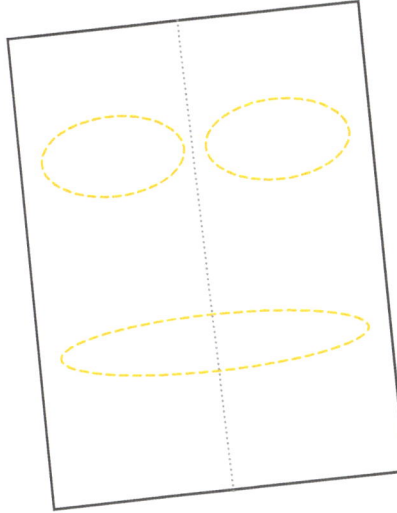

- Take a sheet of paper and cut out eye holes and a mouth hole to create a two-sided mask.
- On one side of paper, draw how you feel when you don't use Happiness Habits regularly, and what can get in the way of daily practice. On the other side, draw how you feel when you use them regularly and how you can work to ensure daily practice of Happiness Habits.

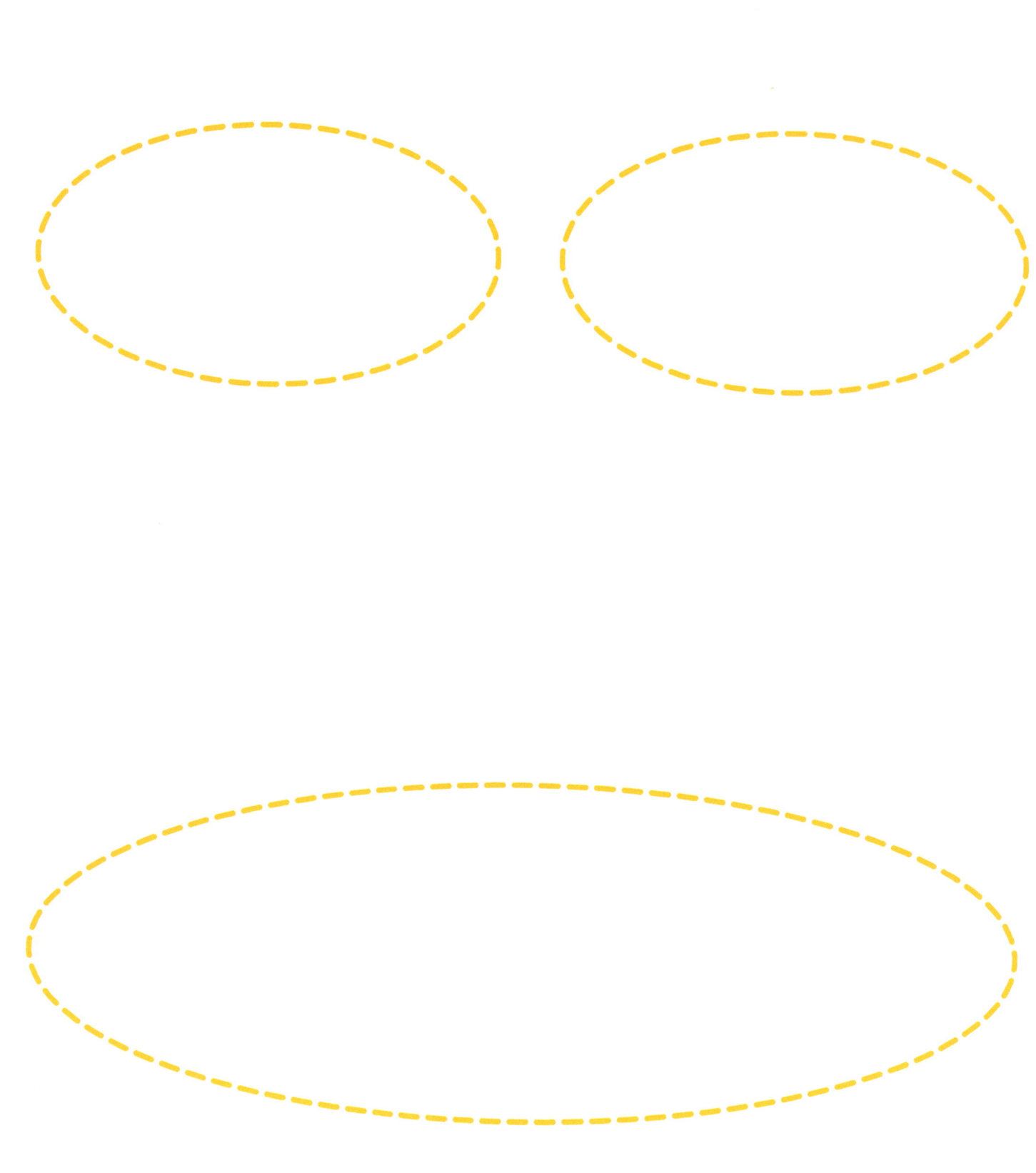

Recap Questions:

What are Happiness Habits, and why are they important?

What is one Happiness Habit you can add to your daily routine and practice each day this week?

How do positive feelings help you work towards your goals?

Lesson 5
Inspired Actions

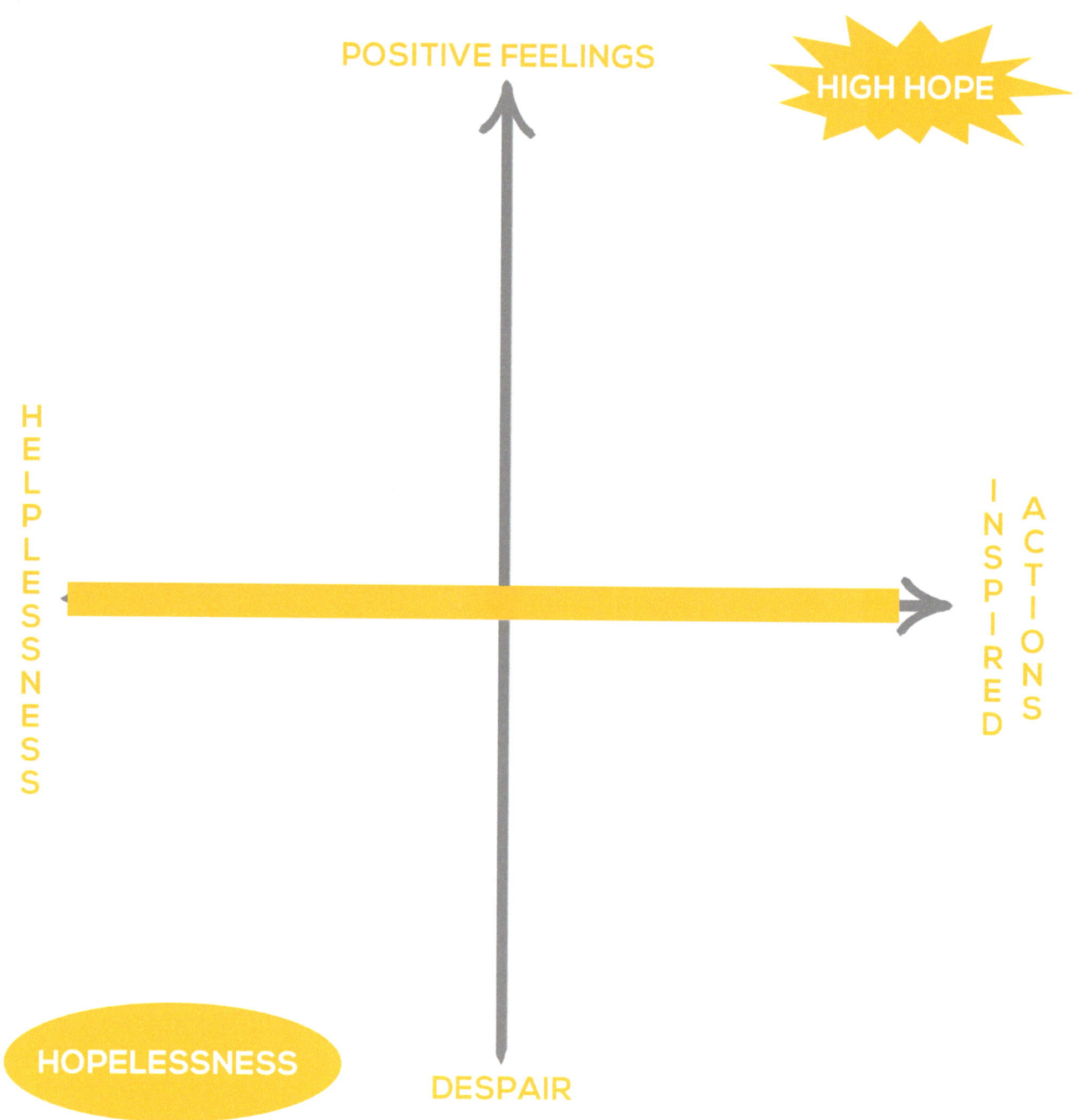

POSITIVE FEELINGS

HIGH HOPE

HELPLESSNESS

INSPIRED ACTIONS

HOPELESSNESS

DESPAIR

Objective

- Understand the importance of goal-setting as it relates to Hope.
- Understand the process for creating SMART goals and potential obstacles.
- Recognize that writing goals down and checking in with someone regularly makes you up to 95% more likely to achieve the goal.

Pre-Questions

Why do you think people set goals?

What challenges might people face when trying to achieve a goal?

What can help someone stay motivated while working towards a goal?

Lesson Instructions

Inspired Actions, the "I" in Shine, are the goal-setting skills that help you set and reach your goals. They help you move from motivational helplessness to Inspired Actions on the Hope Matrix.

Goals are like personal targets that help you improve different areas of your life, such as personal growth, education, career, relationships, and health. They are clear, specific objectives that can be measured and are set within a specific time frame.

Goals are the Inspired Actions we take when we have Hope. Hope is the belief that good things are possible and that a better future is within reach. When we feel hopeful, we are more likely to set goals that align with our passions and interests.

Hope fuels our motivation and optimism, giving us the courage to stay focused and work toward our dreams. When we believe in the possibility of success, we are more likely to take meaningful steps to achieve it.

When brainstorming goals, you can use the WOOP method, which stands for Wish, Outcome, Obstacle, and Plan.

WISH
Think about your purpose. What is the most important wish or concern related to your purpose? Pick a wish that is challenging but that you can still fulfill.

OUTCOME
What would be the best possible outcome if your wish came true? How would fulfilling your wish make you feel?

OBSTACLE
What is within you or in your environment that keeps you from fulfilling your wish?

PLAN
Identify one action you can take or one thought you can think to overcome your obstacle. Then, make an if-then plan: IF (I encounter this obstacle) THEN (I will use this solution).

Using the SMART framework helps ensure your goals are clear and achievable. SMART stands for Specific, Measurable, Attainable, Relevant, and Time-bound. This structure makes tracking progress and staying focused easier, increasing the chances of successfully reaching your goal.

SPECIFIC

Be specific about your goal. Think about these questions when creating your goal: What needs to be accomplished? Who is responsible for it? What steps will you take to achieve it?

MEASURABLE

Can you measure your progress? If this goal will take a long time to achieve, set shorter term goals to reach along the way.

ACHIEVABLE

Are you inspired and motivated to reach your goal? Do you have the tools or skills you need? If not, do you know how you can get them?

RELEVANT

Does your goal make sense? Does it go along with what you are trying to achieve in the bigger picture?

TIME-BOUND

Is your timing realistic? Can you achieve your goal in the time period set? Think about what you may want to achieve at the halfway point.

Another way to work towards goals is to chunk them into microsteps, making the overall goal more manageable. We are 95% more likely to achieve a goal if we write it down and check in with someone regularly about the goal, so it's also important to have someone to help hold you accountable and cheer you on as you make progress.

Physical Activity

Let's practice how to set and implement a SMART goal using an obstacle course challenge.

- Design an obstacle course with different challenges based on available resources. For example, an obstacle course could include stepping over a chair, jumping over an object (i.e., a stone, piece of tape, paper, pen, etc.), balancing while walking on a straight line, or creating a short crawling or bear-walking section. Design a course that allows all group members to participate, keeping everyone's abilities in mind.

- Before starting, have each team create a SMART goal for finishing the course. Have each member of the team walk through the course. The teams can work to complete the obstacle course as many times as needed for them to reach their SMART goal.

- Example SMART goal: Each team member will complete the obstacle course in 5 minutes.
  - **Specific:** Yes
  - **Measurable:** Yes (all of us must do it in under 5 minutes)
  - **Attainable:** Yes, everyone has the capacity
  - **Relevant:** Yes, it is important for all of us to do this.
  - **Time-bound:** Yes, under 5 minutes!

Reflection questions to ask everyone:

- Were there any obstacles you encountered while working to complete your goal? How did you overcome the obstacle?
- How did you feel once your team met the SMART goal?

Arts and Crafts

Have everyone complete the WOOP and SMART goal worksheet.

WISH

OUTCOME

OBSTACLE

PLAN

GOAL:

Is it:

- ◯ **S**PECIFIC?
- ◯ **M**EASURABLE?
- ◯ **A**CHIEVABLE?
- ◯ **R**ELEVANT?
- ◯ **T**IME-BOUND?

Recap Questions:

Why is it important to think of obstacles when setting a goal?

Why is it important to measure progress while working towards a goal?

What makes a goal attainable instead of unrealistic?

Lesson 6
Nourishing Networks

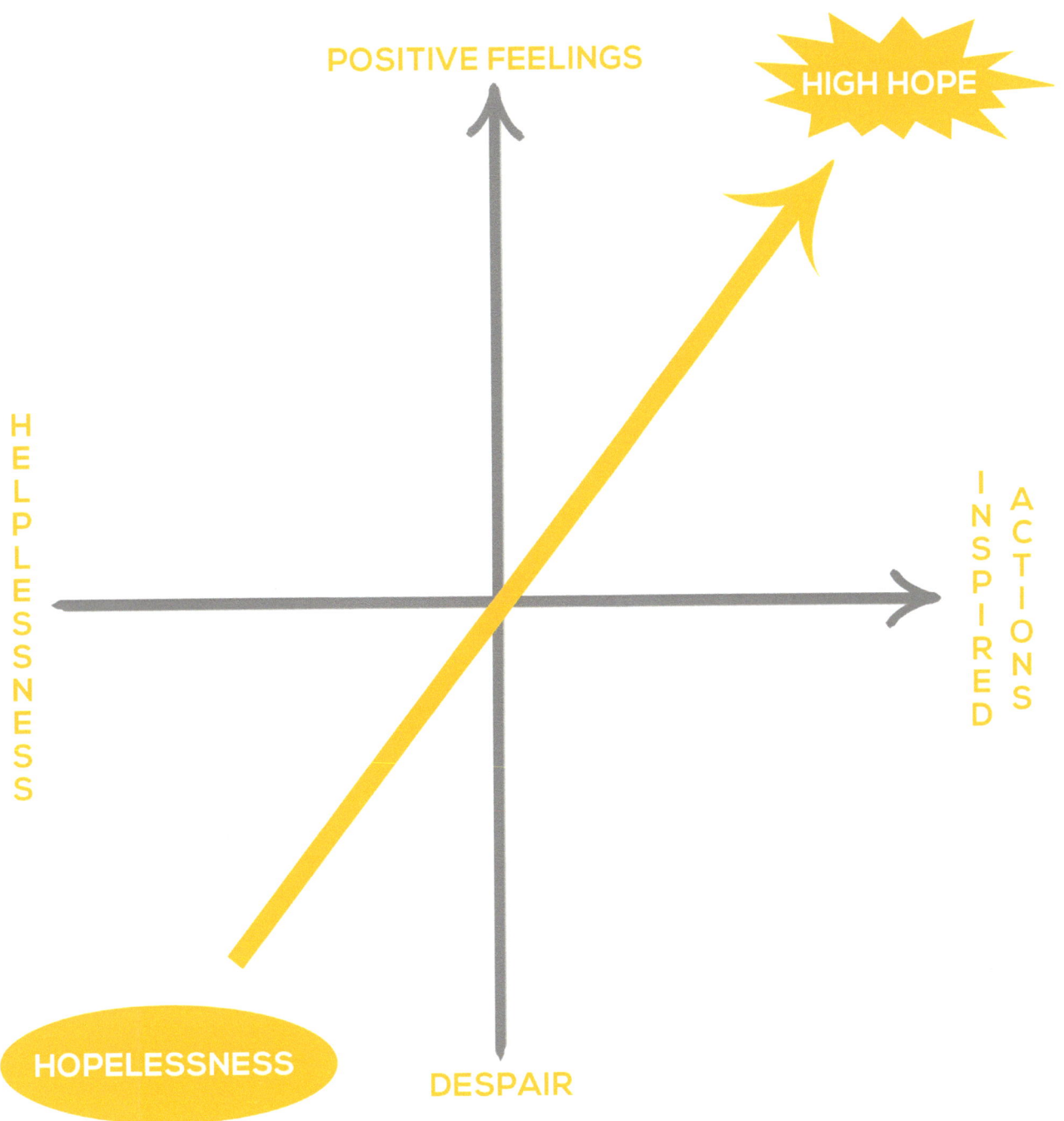

Objectives

- Understand the importance of social connection as it relates to Hope
- Establish your Hope network
- Identify one person in your life you can go to in a time of need

Pre-Questions

What does a Nourishing Network look like to you?

What are some examples of your current Nourishing Network?

What challenges have you faced where someone in your Nourishing Network has helped you?

Lesson Instructions

The Fourth Key to Shine Hope is Nourishing Networks, which are your social support. Building and maintaining a Nourishing Network is critical to Hope. Did you know that socialization can increase positive feelings, and you are 95% more likely to reach a goal if you check in with someone about the goal?

Your Nourishing Networks can include family members, teachers, friends, neighbors, mentors, siblings, doctors, a divine presence, spiritual leaders, loved ones who have passed, Hope heroes, or even pets.

A Nourishing Network is anyone you can turn to whenever you feel hopeless. It is made up of people you trust and who are positive influences in your life.

The goal is to surround yourself with people you trust who will help you through challenging times while supporting you as you work towards your goals. This relationship should be nurtured both ways, as you should support and positively influence your Nourishing Networks in return.

If you currently do not have a Nourishing Network, this is a great opportunity to use the skills learned in the Inspired Actions module to build a Nourishing Network. What goals can you set around creating the network (e.g., finding a mentor, making a new friend, joining a new club, etc.)? What steps must you take to build a Nourishing Network, and how might you feel when you achieve that goal? The worksheet below is an optional tool for building goals around building Nourishing Networks.

Your Hope skills help you overcome challenges to Hope, such as worry, rumination, depression, failure, loneliness, and hopelessness. However, even when your Hope is strong, there are times when you may still need help. Social connection is important for you, just like food and water.

In these activities, you will learn how to support those around you and get support from your peers through trying a pretzel activity with your classmates. You will also identify the people in your life who are a part of your Nourishing Network and places you can go in times of crisis.

Physical Activity

Let's learn how to support and nourish those relationships around you.
- Get into small groups of 5-6 people.
- Stand in a circle, and everyone puts both hands toward the middle of the circle.
- Grab a person's hands across from you and ensure that each of your hand holds hands with different people.
  - Each person should be holding hands with two different people across from them.
- Once everyone is holding hands with someone else, try to untangle yourselves without letting go of your hands.

Reflection questions to ask everyone:
- Did someone specifically help you during this challenge? How did your peers support you in getting untangled?
- How did you support one of your peers in getting untangled? Do you feel like if you were having a real-life challenge one of these people would support you (this can be a teacher who helped give you advice)?

Arts and Crafts

Now, we will design Hope Sunflowers to represent the support systems in our lives.
- Draw a sunflower on a piece of paper or use pre-cut sunflower templates.
- Each petal represents a different type of support—family, friends, mentors, teachers, or community members.
- Write the names of people in your life who support you on the petals.
- Outside of the petals with names, write how that person has supported you and how you can support them.
- In the middle of your sunflower, write where you can go in times of crisis—for instance, the nurse's station at school.
- Decorate your sunflower with colors, symbols, or images that make you feel hopeful and connected.

Recap Questions:

Why is it important to recognize and build a support system? How can having a strong network help you in times of need?

Looking at your Hope Network, which area feels the strongest right now, and which would you like to grow? What are some ways you can strengthen your support network?

Where you can go
in times of crisis?

Lesson 7
Eliminating Challenges

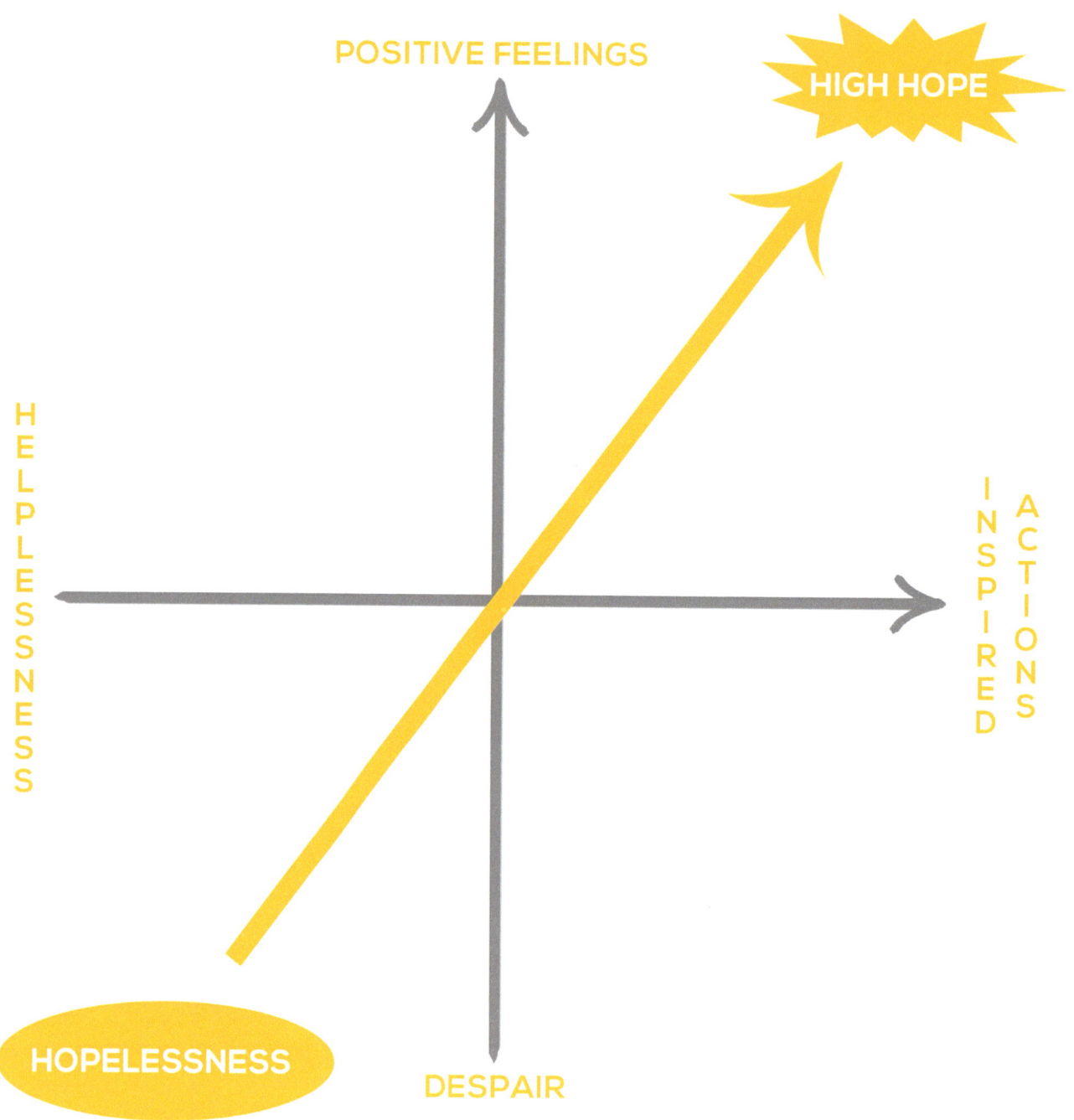

POSITIVE FEELINGS

HIGH HOPE

HELPLESSNESS

INSPIRED ACTIONS

HOPELESSNESS

DESPAIR

Objectives

- Understand that our brain has old thinking patterns, and that we are not our brains!
- Identify three negative thinking patterns to eliminate.
- Prepare which SHINE skills above will be used to eliminate the challenges.

Pre-Questions

What are some negative thinking patterns you have experienced this year? How did they make you feel?

```
┌─────────────────────────────────────────────────────────────────┐
│                                                                   │
│                                                                   │
│                                                                   │
│                                                                   │
│                                                                   │
└─────────────────────────────────────────────────────────────────┘
```

How did you react to those negative thinking patterns? Do you think you learned anything from them?

```
┌─────────────────────────────────────────────────────────────────┐
│                                                                   │
│                                                                   │
│                                                                   │
│                                                                   │
└─────────────────────────────────────────────────────────────────┘
```

Lesson Instructions

The fifth and final key to Shine Hope is Eliminating Challenges, which are the negative thinking patterns that can cause despair and motivational helplessness. It's important to identify ways to manage challenges before they arise so you can quickly and easily move from moments of hopelessness back to Hope.

Automatic negative thoughts are a part of life. These "Challenges to Hope" include negative thinking patterns that make us feel hopeless and helpless. The tricky thing is that these thought patterns are often unconscious, so we don't even realize we're doing them. Once we know what they are and recognize them, we can take action to counteract them.

Some examples of negative thinking habits could include, but are not limited to, limiting beliefs, automatic negative thoughts, rumination, uncontrollables, and internalizing failure. A limiting belief is an example of thinking you're not good enough for something. Automatic Negative Thoughts could be something that automatically pops up in our brains when something happens around us. Rumination is constantly replaying and analyzing past mistakes; uncontrollables are things you focus on that are out of your control. Lastly, internalizing failure is when you take personal responsibility for a setback.

These challenges are bound to happen, but what can we do about them? We can use our Stress Skills, think about evidence that goes against the thought, remember our purpose, and practice our Happiness Habits.

Physical Activity

- **Cut out the cards below. There are two types:**
  - **Role Cards:** Internalizing Failure, Worry, and Rumination.
  - **Scenario Cards:** Real-life situations that could trigger these thinking patterns.
- **Divide into a group of four.**
  - Three people each draw one role card at random.
  - One person draws a scenario card and reads it out loud.
- **Act it out!:** Each person with a role card will respond to the scenario in character, based on their role's thinking pattern.
- **Guess the Role:** After everyone has acted, the group guesses which person was playing which role.
- **Debrief:** Discuss how these thought patterns can impact emotions and behavior, and how they might be challenged or reframed.

ROLE: Internalizing Failure

Everything feels like it's your fault. You think you're not good enough and believe your mistakes define who you are.

ROLE: Worry

You constantly think about what might go wrong. You jump to worst-case scenarios and feel anxious about the future.

ROLE: Rumination

You replay past events over and over in your brain. You focus on your past mistakes and are hard on yourself.

SCENARIO
You didn't get picked for the team.

SCENARIO
Your friend didn't text you back.

SCENARIO
You failed a math test.

SCENARIO
You said something awkward in class.

SCENARIO
You were late turning in your homework.

SCENARIO
You got into an argument with a sibling.

SCENARIO
_____
_____

SCENARIO
_____
_____

SCENARIO
_____
_____

SCENARIO
_____
_____

SCENARIO
_____
_____

SCENARIO
_____
_____

SCENARIO
_____
_____

SCENARIO
_____
_____

SCENARIO
_____
_____

Arts and Crafts

- Draw a picture of a time you experienced a moment of hopelessness.
- Write down which negative thinking pattern you experienced during that time.
- Crinkle up your paper and open it back up. In all of the creases of your paper, write down different ways to eliminate the challenge you wrote about above.
- You can add your personal touch by using colorful markers or drawing pictures.
- Remember, everyone faces obstacles and none of us can control everything. These cracks represent the fact that you can learn a lot from challenges you face if you remember the ways to eliminate them.

Recap Questions:

Do you feel differently about the negative thinking patterns you wrote down in the pre-questions? If you could go back, what would you do differently?

In what ways will you Eliminate Challenges in the future?

Lesson 8
My Shine Hope Story

Objectives

- Understand how to draw a My Shine Hope Story.
- Know the skills to teach others to draw their My Shine Hope Story.
- Plan three ways to continue building Hope skills.

Pre-Questions

Can you think of a difficult time or challenge you've worked through?

[ ]

How did you feel after navigating this challenge?

[ ]

Can you think of a challenge you've watched someone in your life work through?

[ ]

Lesson Instructions

My Shine Hope Story is designed to give individuals a framework for getting through challenges in their lives. This framework can be viewed as a guide for future struggles and shared with others to inspire Hope and provide new ways to navigate challenges. My Shine Hope Story is one tool to help us tap into the "action" portion of Hope, moving past simply visualizing a better future and identifying tangible steps we can take to get there.

The My Shine Hope Story focuses minimally on the challenge you chose *(only about 20% of the content should be about the challenge)* and mainly focuses on strategies to overcome it *(80% of the content should focus on this).*

Individuals choose to represent the keys to SHINE Hope creatively in whatever way inspires them.

Physical Activity

- Create a "gallery walk" in whatever space your group is in. Look at other people's stories, however they chose to represent them (whether through drawing, painting, or acting them out). Give each person time to share their story and take time to see each person's. Their story can help you navigate challenges in your future!

Arts and Crafts

- Using paper or whatever crafting materials are available, start to create your My Shine Hope Story. (Next Page)

Recap Questions:

How did it feel to reflect on a challenge you have overcome?

What is one thing you took away from looking at someone else's story?

How can you use your story to help you when you face another challenge in the future?

☀ MY SHINE HOPE STORY™

HOW HOPEFUL ARE YOU?

Did you measure your hope? The lower your score, the more you want to practice these skills! Remember, hope is a muscle we need to build it (add it).

Check out here to get your hope score.

To write your own shine hope story, spend 20% of your time writing about your challenge, and 80% of the time sharing strategies for how you overcame it so others can learn from you. Here's how:

 1. Write your name on the yellow line next to the box (feel free to use a nickname or anything else).

2. Put your favorite photo in the yellow box, or an image of something that represents you.

3. Write an introduction to your story explaining the challenge you faced. Explain the two ingredients of hopelessness: despair (feelings) and helplessness (inability to act) you experienced.

 4. Share sadness, anger, fear, or other feelings, and choose **3 Stress Skills** you used to naviate them (from the Shine infographic, or choose your own!).

 5. Share **3 Happiness Habits** you used to get back to your upstairs brain.

 6. Talk about **3 Inspired Actions** you took, or share how you chunked down goals, the types of goals you set, or if you had to regoal.

 7. Share who was in your **Nourishing Network**, and how they helped you navigate the challenge.

 8. Pick 3 challenges from the '**Eliminating Challenges**' on the infographic, and share how you eliminated them.

 9. Write your conclusion. What do you want the world to know? What do you wish someone had told you? What is the moral of the story?

If you're inspired, share your story so we can help activate these skills globally.

#Hope #ShineHope #MyShineHopeStory

We all experience moments of hopelessness (emotional despair and motivational helplessness). The key is to use the Shine Hope skills to navigate your way from despair to positive feelings, and helplessness to inspired actions. Use the Shine Hope framework to build your muscle.

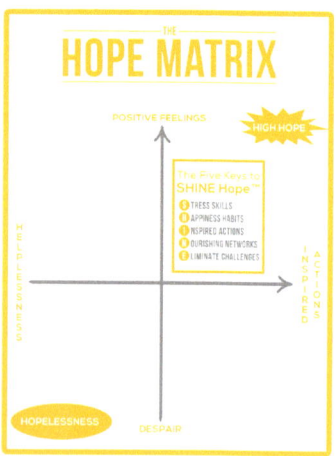

MY SHINE HOPE STORY™

☀ Kathryn Goetzke

When I was 18 years old, a freshman at the University of Iowa, I called home and heard an unfamiliar, deep voice on the other line. It wasn't anyone I recognized, and he asked for my mom. My mom got on the phone to tell me my dad had taken his life. In that instance, my whole world crumbled. I felt a sadness so deep I thought I would never survive, and a helplessness so profound as I could not bring him back.

As hard as it was, I had to move forward. I started using Stress Skills to manage my pain. I cried when I was sad, started boxing to manage my anger, and learned how to start belly breathing to manage my fear. I listened to a lot of calming music when things got hard, and I started hiking all over the world. I also learned how to use sensory engagement to bring myself to the present moment.

Happiness Habits were critical. Sleep became an important part of my routine, and I started eating healthier foods. I cut alcohol out of my life. I replaced smoking with running, and made comedy clubs and laughter a part of my life. I listened to music, turned my sensory engagement passion into a purpose and started a company, and made volunteering a regular part of my life. I used dancing and live concerts (like my fave The Killers) as a form of release.

I also was very intentional about Inspired Actions. I had to chunk down my goals, leaving school and taking only one year at a time until I graduated. I had to regoal from having experiences with my dad to finding father-like figures to be in my life. I got closer to my brothers, their kids, and found mentors like Paul Carter and Dr. Belfer to guide me on my journey. My mom is my rock, my greatest source of strength and inspiration, keeping me moving forward towards my dreams.

Nourishing Networks were a constant. I stayed close to my friends and family, traveling, dancing, studying, and laughing. They were so compassionate, kind, generous, fun, and helped me heal. I forgave my dad for leaving, and forgave myself for not being there for him when he needed me. I got very close to God, understanding that I couldn't save my dad, and that in time this lesson would teach me how to help others.

It wasn't easy to Eliminate Challenges like rumination, internalizing failure, or worry. Yet I studied sensory engagement to be present when my mind started running. I deconstructed what led to my dad taking his life in a way that made it clear how to save myself and others. I knew that I couldn't control my dad, just like I can't control others. So I have focused on creating programming yet not being attached to if people want to learn it.

It's not been the easiest journey, and takes work. Yet by using the Shine Hope framework I have created a new life that is full of wonder, awe, happiness, adventure, and meaning. A different one than I expected, yet a beautiful one because I was able to dive in my pain, and learn the lessons necessary to teach others. And I use all my dad taught me in business to create a Shine Hope model for the world that ensures all know the what, why, and how of hope. And for that I know he is so very proud.

No matter what life brings, Keep Shining.

#Hope #ShineHope #MyHopeStory

the shine hope company

MY SHINE HOPE STORY™

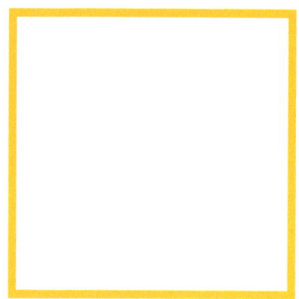

CHILDREN AND STRESS

Stress is the product of the demands that are placed on us, and a normal part of life. It is not stress that kills us, it is our inability to effectively manage stress. Friends, family, jobs, or school can create stress, as well as a disconnection between what we think we should be accomplishing and what we are actually able to accomplish.

Children are not immune to stress, and if your child is feeling stress they are not alone. Some research suggests children are even more stressed than adults in these times. There are many reasons your children may encounter stress. Our Hopeful Minds program addresses stress, and provides stress management techniques, including the key 90 second rule. Our goal is to share additional insights, and provide tips on what else you might do at home.

As children grow, academic and social pressures, world news, and external trauma can become stressors at an increasing rate. The symptoms of stress can vary; however, the following list contains some of the more common symptoms typically identified in children suffering from stress:

- Stomachaches
- Headaches and Nightmares
- Trouble concentrating or completing schoolwork
- Overreacting to minor problems
- Becoming clingy
- Becoming withdrawn or spending more time alone
- Short-term behavioral changes, such as mood swings, acting out, bedwetting, and changes in sleep pattern
- Younger children may start thumb sucking, hair twirling, and nose picking
- Older children may begin lying, bullying, or defying authority
- Drastic changes in academic performance

SOLUTIONS TO STRESS

There are healthy ways to help children both cope with and minimize stressors in their lives. We've provided a number of solutions in our Hopeful Minds program, and encourage you to do it with them so they start to recognize "stress," know how it feels in their body, and proactively manage it. It isn't stress that hurts us, it is our inability to manage stress. In addition to practicing Hope strategies with them, you can support your child in managing their stress in the following ways:

AT HOME

- Download our Parent's Guide at www.hopefulminds.org/curriculums, and start using Hope language at home.
- Make sure your child is getting proper rest and nutrition. Children need a well-balanced diet and 9-12 hours of sleep each night to stay physically and mentally healthy.
- Ensure your home is a physically and emotionally safe place for your child to come home to.
- Commit to a routine.
- Monitor the amount of screen time, as well as the television, video game, and book content your child is ingesting. The following two articles give excellent insights into the problems that can arise from too much screen time during childhood.
    - https://gabb.com/blog/how-smart-phones-affect-brain-development/
    - https://gabb.com/blog/austin-weirichs-story/
- Don't overschedule. Too many extracurricular activities can increase stress.
- Take time to talk through changes with your child before they happen.
- Encourage children to perform visualization and breathing activities prior to stressful events, such as games and tests.
- Learn to listen to problems without being critical or solving the problems for them. Help your children find their own solutions to situations that are adding stress to their lives.

- At the start of conversations with your children, establish whether they want you to listen, give advice, or take action based on the information they are sharing.
- Provide affection and encouragement.
- Adopt healthy habits, such as exercise and self-care, to manage your own stress in healthy ways. Children are perceptive and will pick up on how you react to your own stressors.

AT SCHOOL

- Involve students in social, club, and athletic activities where they can succeed.
- Use positive reinforcement and methods of discipline that promote self-esteem.
- Limit homework overload.
- Take time to actively listen to students and help them find ways to decrease stressors in their lives.
- Use frequent "movement" breaks between lessons to keep students active and engaged.
- Schedule time to organize. Especially in lower grades, providing time to organize desks and cubbies, sharpen pencils, and put away toys and tools can give students a greater sense of control.
- Establish a routine and implement your own time management techniques. A hectic classroom schedule is a common stressor for students.
- Encourage students to perform visualization and breathing activities prior to stressful events, such as games and tests.
- Pay attention to behavioral changes in your students. If concerning behaviors are continually exhibited, reach out to parents and/or a counselor.
- Provide patience and encouragement.

CHILDREN AND ANXIETY

When stress is not properly mitigated, it can lead to anxiety. Anxiety disorders negatively impact a child's life in many ways. Most children have fears and worries that appear at different times during development. Although fears and worries are normal, persistent or extreme fears may be due to anxiety.

The general rule is if any of these symptoms appear for two or more weeks, and are disrupting your child's daily life and activities, it is best to seek advice from a medical professional. The following is a list of symptoms that may help you determine if your child is experiencing anxiety:

- Distress during separation
- Phobias
- Fear and discomfort in social settings
- Excessive worry about the future and bad things happening
- Abnormal irritation or anger
- Trouble sleeping and fatigue
- Headaches and Stomachaches
- Repeated episodes of sudden, unexpected fear that come with symptoms such as heart pounding, trouble breathing, feeling dizzy, shaking, and sweating

MANAGING ANXIETY

As a parent or teacher, your goal isn't to eliminate a child's anxiety, but to help them learn to manage it. If you believe your child may have anxiety, it is important to take active steps to get your child the help they need including talking to a medical professional like your primary care doctor, or a therapist.

There is no shame in seeking support. Just as you would encourage your child to get support for heart or lung issues, kids need to feel comfortable seeking help for their brain. Mental health is a unique interplay of behavioral and biological exchange, so it is important to work on both. You can help them manage their anxiety in the following ways:

AT HOME

- Consult with your child's pediatrician or family physician. A mental health assessment and evaluation can be done for a diagnosis and treatment plan. Your doctor may refer you to a mental health professional such as a psychiatrist, psychologist, or counselor. (Do not delay treatment. Early detection and diagnosis are important for getting your child the help they need. Though parents or guardians can often feel responsible for what is happening with their children, they did not cause the anxiety.)

- Respect your child's feelings but don't empower the feelings. It is important to acknowledge that their feelings are real and valid and help them find the source of the anxiety they are feeling. However, once they have acknowledged their anxiety, it is important to help children learn to face their fears. Make sure you are not reinforcing fears with your behaviors.

- Make sure your child is getting proper rest and nutrition. Children need a well-balanced diet and 9-12 hours of sleep each night to stay physically and mentally healthy.

- Ensure your home is a physically and emotionally safe place for your child to come home to.

- Commit to a routine.

- Monitor the amount of screen time, as well as the television, video game, and book content your child is ingesting.

- Practice mindfulness and relaxation techniques.

- Take time to talk through changes with your child before they happen. Preparing for upcoming changes can help remove the anxiety associated with them.

- At the start of conversations with your children, establish whether they want you to listen, give advice, or take action based on the information they are sharing.

- Help your child with problem-solving skills. Develop a plan of realistic steps your child can take toward a goal, recognize their success on the path, and encourage the enjoyment of the experience along the way. Help identify potential obstacles or difficulties and plan/talk about ways to overcome them. Focus on strengths.

- Adopt healthy habits to manage your own anxieties. Children are perceptive and will pick up on how you react to your own anxieties.
- Have conversations with your children about failure. It is important for them to understand that everyone fails at things and that when they fail, it does not mean that they are failures.

AT SCHOOL

- Use positive reinforcement and methods of discipline that promote self-esteem.
- Respect your student's feelings but don't empower the feelings. It is important to acknowledge that their feelings are valid and help them find the source of the anxiety they are feeling. However, once they have acknowledged their anxiety, it is important to help children learn to face their fears. Make sure you are not reinforcing fears with your behaviors.
- Limit homework overload.
- Take time to actively listen to students and help them find ways to decrease stressors in their lives.
- Schedule time to organize. Especially in lower grades, providing time to organize desks and cubbies, sharpen pencils, and put away toys and tools can give students a greater sense of control.
- Encourage students to face their anxieties in baby steps. Come up with techniques that allow them to participate a bit more each time.
- Establish a routine and implement your own time management techniques. A hectic classroom schedule is a common stressor for students.
- Encourage students to perform visualization and breathing activities prior to stressful events, such as games and tests.
- Pay attention to student interactions to prevent bullying and abuse within your classroom.
- Pay attention to behavioral changes in your students. If concerning behaviors are continually exhibited, check your school's policy and reach out to parents, guardians and/or a counselor.
- Provide patience and encouragement.
- Have conversations with your students about failure. It is important for them to understand that everyone fails at things and that when they fail, it does not mean that they are failures.

CHILDREN AND DEPRESSION

Depression is a serious mood disorder that can take the joy from a child's life. It is normal for a child to be moody or sad from time to time. However, if these feelings last more than two weeks, and start to interfere with daily activities, it may be a sign of clinical depression. The following list of symptoms may help you identify if a child is experiencing depression.

- Frequent sadness, or crying more often or more easily
- Poor concentration
- Increased irritability, anger, or hostility
- Hopelessness
- Decreased interest in activities, or an inability to enjoy usual activities
- Persistent boredom or low energy
- Social isolation/withdrawal: Spending more time alone, away from family and friends
- Violence towards self or others
- "Clingy" and more dependent behavior in certain relationships
- Overly pessimistic attitude or excessive guilt
- Feelings of worthlessness and extreme sensitivity to rejection or failure
- Difficulty with relationships
- Over or under eating, or any form of addictive behavior
- Frequent complaints of physical illnesses, such as headaches and stomachaches
- Frequent absences from school or poor performance in school
- Major changes in eating and/or sleeping patterns
- Talk of, or efforts to, run away from home
- Self-destructive behavior or self-harm
- Thoughts of death or expressions of suicide
- Increase in risk-taking behaviors and/or showing less concern for their own safety
- Younger children may act younger than their age (regression)
- Low self-esteem

MANAGING DEPRESSION

Depression may look different in a child than in an adult, and therefore many children do not get the treatment they need. If you believe your child may be depressed, it is important to take active steps to get your child the help they need. You can help them manage their depression in the following ways:

AT HOME

- Consult with your child's pediatrician or family physician. A mental health assessment and evaluation can be done for a diagnosis and treatment plan. Your doctor may refer you to a mental health professional such as a psychiatrist, psychologist, or counselor. (Do not delay treatment. Early detection and diagnosis are important for getting your child the help they need. Though parents can often feel responsible for what is happening with their children, they did not cause the depression.)

- Respect your child's feelings but don't empower the feelings. It is important to acknowledge that their feelings are real and valid and help them find the source of the anxiety they are feeling. However, once they have acknowledged their anxiety, it is important to help children learn to face their fears. Make sure you are not reinforcing fears with your behaviors.

- Make sure your child is getting proper rest and nutrition. Children need a well-balanced diet and 9-12 hours of sleep each night to stay physically and mentally healthy.

- Life stressors such as an illness, a separation/divorce, a move, or death can trigger short-term problems or lead to depression. Under these stressors, it is helpful for families to turn to a mental health professional. Depression is treatable, but, if left untreated, can be life threatening. Depression is a major risk factor for suicide.

- Communicate with your child's school. Teachers, school psychologists, and social workers are there to help.

- Talk to your child and listen carefully. Never dismiss feelings, but point out realities and offer Hope.

- Remind your child that you are always there to help and support them. Depressed children need continual reassurance. It is common for them to feel unworthy when experiencing depression.
- Remind your child that they are important and needed.
- Encourage and be a positive role model for a healthy lifestyle. Getting proper nutrition, having adequate sleep, and exercising all help alleviate stress, build relationships, and improve mood.
- Help your child with problem-solving skills. Develop a plan of realistic steps your child can take toward a goal, recognize their success on the path, and encourage the enjoyment of the experience along the way. Help identify potential obstacles or difficulties and plan/talk about ways to overcome them. Focus on strengths.
- Never ignore statements and comments about death or suicide. Report them to your child's doctor immediately and if you believe your child is in immediate danger do not leave them alone. Contact your local emergency room in the US; or numbers at the end of this document. You may develop a safety and emergency plan of your own. Have a list of numbers ready to call.

AT SCHOOL

- Communicate with the student's parents, as well as the school psychologists and social workers.
- Talk to your student and listen carefully. Never dismiss feelings, but point out realities and offer Hope.
- Use positive reinforcement and methods of discipline that promote self-esteem.
- Use frequent "movement" breaks between lessons to keep students active and engaged. Exercise can help decrease depression and increase mindfulness.
- Schedule time to organize. Especially in lower grades, providing time to organize desks and cubbies, sharpen pencils, and put away toys and tools can give students a greater sense of control.
- Establish a routine and implement your own time management techniques. A hectic classroom schedule can be an additional stressful obstacle for students to deal with.
- Remind your student that you are always there to help and support them. Depressed children need continual reassurance. It is common for them to feel unworthy when experiencing depression.

- Help your student with problem-solving skills. Develop a plan of realistic steps your student can take toward an academic goal, recognize their success on the path, and encourage the enjoyment of the experience along the way. Help identify potential obstacles or difficulties and plan/talk about ways to overcome them. Focus on strengths.v

- Never ignore statements and comments about death or suicide. Report them to the school counselor and the student's parents immediately. If you believe your student is in immediate danger do not leave them alone. Contact your local emergency room in the US; or numbers at the end of this document. You may develop a safety and emergency plan of your own. Have a list of numbers ready to call.

RESEARCH CITED

The information provided in this document was obtained from the following sources:

1. Childhood Stress. Kidshealth.org (updated February 2015).
2. Stress in School. Community for Accredited Online Schools (updated 2019).
3. Anxiety and Depression in Children, CDC Children's Mental Health (updated March 30, 2020).
4. What to Do (and Not Do) When Children are Anxious, Child Mind Institute.
5. How to Help a Child Struggling with Anxiety. NPR (published October 29, 2019).
6. Depression in Children and Teens. Web MD (updated May 2013).
7. Medical Reference from Healthwise, Incorporated.
8. Adolescent Depression: What Parents Can Do To Help.
9. HealthyChildren.org (updated February 2018).

Where to Find Support

U.S. SUICIDE HOTLINES AND IMMEDIATE TELEPHONE SUPPORT

If you or someone you know needs immediate help in the U.S., call any of the lines for Hope below to talk to someone in your local area. They can listen to you and direct you to local resources if further assistance is needed. If someone has talked to you about suicide, and you believe they are currently a threat to themselves or someone else but won't take your help, call 911.

988	United States Crisis Hotline. Hours: Available 24 hours. Languages: English, Spanish.
(888)628-9454	National Suicide Prevention Lifeline: Spanish Language Available
(800)799-4889	National Suicide Prevention Lifeline: Deaf & Hard of Hearing Options
(800)784-2432	1-800-SUICIDA Spanish Speaking Suicide Hotline
(877)968-8454	1-877-YOUTHLINE Teen to Teen Peer Counseling Hotline
(866)488-7386	TrevorLifeLine for LGBTQ Support
(877)565-8860	Trans Lifeline

You can also text HOME to 741741 to connect with a crisis counselor from crisistextline.org.

If you are in need of support, you can find additional resources by visiting www.ifred.org/individual-support or scanning the QR Code.

TO FIND A LIST OF INTERNATIONAL RESOURCES VISIT:
www.ifred.org/resources

SHINE HOPE™

A HOW-TO FOR HOPE IN TRYING TIMES

STRESS SKILLS	**H**APPINESS HABITS	**I**NSPIRED ACTIONS	**N**OURISHING NETWORKS	**E**LIMINATING CHALLENGES
90 second pause	Activating purpose	WOOP process	5:1 Rule	Limiting beliefs
Belly breathing	Pursuing passion	SMART goals	Compassion	Automatic Negative Thoughts (ANTs)
Journaling	Utilizing strengths	Stretch goals	Forgiveness	All-or-nothing thinking
Gardening	Meditation	Achievement goals	Love	Negative bias
Calming music	Smiling	Intrinsic goals	Gratitude	Rumination & Worry
Affirming beliefs	Exercising / Nutrition	Mastery goals	Recognition	Focusing on Uncontrollables
Sensory engagement	Creating / listening to music	Micro goals /Stepping	Support	Attaching to outcomes
Cold plunge	Dancing / Singing	Habit Stacking	Faith	Internalizing failure
Decluttering	Drawing / Painting	Visualization	Trust	Toxic Consumption
Prayer	Gratitude	Overcoming obstacles	Respect	Nocebo Effect
Nature walk	Volunteering	Regoaling	Effective Listening	Mind Wandering
Napping	Wonder / Awe	Write down goals / check in	Empathy	Implicit Bias
Laughter	Quality sleep		Kindness	Negative Framing
Crying	Doodling		Animals	Perfectionism Taking
Tapping				things personally
Yoga				
Mantras				

the **shine hope**™ company

STRESS SKILLS

Stress Skills are actions that help you navigate your stress response and work through your body's chemical response to external stimuli. By practicing them, you are teaching yourself how to proactively manage the emotional despair found in hopelessness and move toward positive feelings where you activate Hope.

The Stress Response

This is when you are emotionally triggered by something in your environment, and you go into fight, flight, freeze, or fawn mode as your body releases stress hormones, such as cortisol, adrenaline, and norepinephrine. You are in your downstairs brain, and can't reach your upstairs brain; the upstairs brain is the place where you make good decisions for moving toward all you Hope for in life.

90 second pause	Sensory engagement	Laughter
Belly breathing	Cold plunge	Crying
Journaling	Decluttering	Tapping
Gardening	Prayer	Yoga
Calming music	Nature walk	Mantras
Affirming beliefs	Napping	

HAPPINESS HABITS

Happiness Habits are healthy, long-term actions that cause your brain to release happiness hormones including endorphins, dopamine, serotonin, and oxytocin. Happiness Habits help you stay in your upstairs brain, where you access the problem-solving skills, collaboration, and passion critical for Hope.

Positive Feelings

Positive feelings, the first ingredient of Hope, are feelings that are located in your upstairs brain like wonder, joy, and peace that make it easier to overcome obstacles that get in the way of Hope. You proactively manage the emotional despair of hopelessness using Stress Skills and use your Happiness Habits to stay in your upstairs brain, where you then energetically move toward your goals in life.

Activating purpose	Exercising / Nutrition	Volunteering
Pursuing passion	Creating / listening to music	Wonder / Awe
Utilizing strengths	Dancing / Singing	Quality sleep
Meditation	Drawing / Painting	Doodling
Smiling	Gratitude	

INSPIRED ACTIONS

Inspired Actions, the second ingredient of Hope, are the deliberate steps you take toward your goals in life. Inspired Actions help you to move away from the motivational helplessness, the second ingredient of hopelessness, and toward what you are Hopeful for in life.

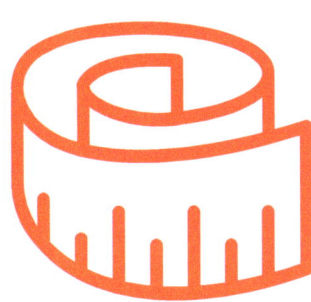

Types of Goals:

WOOP   SMART

Achievement   Stretch

Intrinsic   Micro-Goals

Pathways, Agency, and Regoaling

Obstacles are inevitable, and sometimes you can't reach the goal as you intended. It is important to embrace obstacles to goals, learn to pivot or reevaluate, be flexible and adaptable, and never be afraid to ask for help.

If a goal seems too big, use the stepping process or create micro-goals to chunk it down into smaller goals. Think of one thing you can do in the next 20 minutes. And know when you need to re-goal.

NOURISHING NETWORKS

Your Nourishing Networks, also known as your Hope Networks, are the people in your life that provide you with support, help you stay on track, encourage you to succeed, and who you do the same for in return. You are up to 95% more likely to achieve a goal if you write it down, and check in with someone regularly. So Nourishing Networks are critical support systems for moving you toward what you Hope for in life.

Your Hope Networks should include:

People who know and understand you.

People who value your strengths.

People who activate the SHINE framework.

People whom you trust and can confide in.

People who are available to support you.

People you are willing to do the above for as well.

Enhancing Your Hope Networks

Enhance your Hope Networks using the 5:1 rule, vulnerability, praise, recognition, kindness, gratitude, empathy, compassion, collaboration, and strong communication, and be sure to have different networks for different areas of life.

Don't forget to include doctors, therapists, and/or other medical professionals in your Hope Networks.

E LIMINATING CHALLENGES

Challenges to Hope are negative habits of thought that quickly take you to hopelessness, that emotional despair and sense of helplessness. The thought patterns are often unconscious habits, so becoming aware of these patterns is critical. Once we know what they are and recognize them, it is important to counteract them so that we don't let them keep us from all we Hope for in life.

Eliminating Challenges

Most of the Challenges to Hope take constant, repetitive actions to change and overcome. Thanks to the science of neuroplasticity, we know it is possible with practice and dedication. The key is to learn to identify what specific challenges happen most frequently and then proactively find ways to manage those challenges.

Limiting beliefs	Focusing on Uncontrollables	Mind Wandering
Automatic Negative Thoughts (ANTs)	Attaching to outcomes	Implicity Bias
All-or-nothing thinking	Internalizing failure	Negative Framing
Negative bias	Toxic Consumption	Perfectionism Taking
Rumination & Worry	Nocebo Effect	things personally

Additional Resources

Hopeful Minds is based on the research that hope is teachable. The aim is to equip all students, teachers, and parents with the tools they need to define, learn, and grow a Hopeful Mind. The Hopeful Minds curriculums and resources are available for download at www.hopefulminds.org/curriculums

The Five-Day Global Hope Challenge is a daily challenge that introduces the Five Keys to Shine Hope that everyone can use to activate hope within their lives and their community. The challenge is ideal for governments, workplaces, schools, and more. Sign-up today at www.hopefulcities.org

Friendship Bench's mission is to get people out of kufungisisa - depression & anxiety - by creating safe spaces and a sense of belonging in communities to improve mental wellbeing and enhance quality of life. To learn more and request a bench placed in your area, visit www.friendshipbenchzimbabwe.org

Karma Box Project is a community initiative allowing people to give non-perishable food, hygiene products, toiletries, and other useful items to those in need. The boxes are filled up with the goods by anyone in the community and someone in need can take items from the box as needed. To learn more, visit www.karmaboxproject.org

One World Strong Foundation created the ResilienceNet Mobile App, which empowers and provides support to local, regional, and national terrorism prevention practitioners, relevant frontline responders and individual Americans seeking support. To learn more about the One World Strong Foundation and download their app, visit www.oneworldstrong.org/copy-of-how-we-do-it

National Alliance on Mental Illness (NAMI) is America's largest grassroots mental health organization dedicated to building better lives for Americans affected by mental illness. NAMI offers an abundance of resources for those navigating mental illness or for those seeking to learn more.
Find more at www.nami.org/home

Choose Love Movement nurtures safer and more loving communities through next generation essential life skills and character development programs for all stages of life. Choose Love is an evidence-based curriculum that will help students feel safer, learn better, and achieve more! Find out more at www.chooselovemovement.org

Hope Means Nevada works to eliminate teen suicide and empower Nevada's youth to live hopeful lives. Find out more at www.hopemeansnevada.org

One Mind catalyzes visionary change through science, business and media to transform the world's mental health. Find out more at www.onemind.org

Charter for Compassion supports the emerging global movement that brings compassion to life. It is a global network connecting people, cities, grassroots organizers and leaders to each other. It provides educational resources, organizing tools, and avenues for communication. Find out more at www.charterforcompassion.org

CDC NATIONAL HEALTH EDUCATION STANDARDS

The National Health Education Standards (NHES) were developed to establish, promote, and support health-enhancing behaviors for students in all grade levels—from pre-Kindergarten through grade 12. The NHES provides a framework for teachers, administrators, and policy makers in designing or selecting curricula, allocating instructional resources, and assessing student achievement and progress. Importantly, the standards provide students, families and communities with concrete expectations for health education.

ILLINOIS STATE STANDARDS FOR SOCIAL/EMOTIONAL LEARNING CURRICULUM ALIGNMENT

The state of Illinois defines social and emotional learning as "the process through which children and adults acquire knowledge, attitudes, and skills they need to:"

- Recognize and manage their emotions
- Demonstrate caring and concern for others
- Establish positive relationships
- Make responsible decisions
- Handle challenging situations constructively

Further, "Quality SEL instruction in which students learn to process, integrate, and selectively apply SEL skills in developmentally, contextually, and culturally appropriate ways in conjunction with a safe, caring, participatory and responsive school climate can result in positive outcomes including:"

- Promotion of mental wellness
- Prevention of mental health issues
- School connectedness
- Reduction in student absenteeism
- Reduction in suspensions
- Adoption, implementation, and institutionalization of new practices
- Improved academic outcomes

You can check www.hopefulminds.org/curriculums and download our guide that reviews how for each lesson for the Overview and Deep Dive programs meet these CDC guidelines.